WOMANHOOD
BREAK FREE FROM THE WORLD'S DESIGN. IT IS KILLING YOU!

Virtuous by Design

All rights reserved.

This book or any portion thereof may not be reproduced or used in any manner whatsoever without the express written permission of the publisher except for the use of brief quotations in a book review or scholarly journal. Please contact author for permission.

© 2009. Khalilah Cole, Evelisse Curbelo, Rosemary Devers, Patricia Jefferson, Lonna Swann, and Robin Sykes. All rights reserved.

ISBN 978-0-359-75982-8
Biblically Speaking Publication
PO BOX 121545 Clermont, FL 34712
www.VirtuousByDesign.org

Scripture quotations marked (NIV) are taken from the Holy Bible, New International Version. copyright © 1996, 2004, 2007 by Tyndale House Foundation. Used by permission of Tyndale House Publishers, Inc., Carol Stream, Illinois 60188. All rights reserved.

INTRODUCTION
By
Robin Sykes

As a woman that God created, we are prized and cherished. We are adored. We are loved beyond measure. We are cared for deeply, delighted in, and treasured. God loves us too and nothing can separate us from that (**Romans 8:31-39**). We were not an afterthought. He enjoys women and treasures them like a proud father. That's how God feels about His women. God created us in His own image.

We are a masterpiece designed by the most skillful artisan the world has ever known **(Psalm 139:14)**. We have opinions and ideas that are valuable. We are worth listening to even when the man's "Adam experience" tells him not to. Our input and creativity make a difference.

No matter where we have come from, who we have been, or what we have down, our story is valuable and sharing our story, using our voice to honor God, is a beautiful thing and required for us to overcome. We are uniquely called by God. Just like Queen Esther, Judge Deborah and the mother of Jesus...so are you... **YOU ARE WORTHY AND WORTH IT!!!**
-Robin Sykes

This book is for the single woman, the married woman, the woman married to an unbelieving spouse, the woman who is just ready to move into her winning season and break free from the cycles. If you have found yourself to be bitter, angry for no reason at the wrong people, broken, beat down, beat up, dismayed, lost, lonely, alone, unappreciated, cast away, lied on, talked about, gossiping, confused, caught up in drama, misused, abused, unable to heal, unloved, unaccepted, unprotected, loose, restless, relentless, insatiable, wandering, or just plain friendless...this book is for you. As woman we were created to be relational and God made us to be more than what a man could ever be alone. It is your time to take your place. You will not only build those in your household, but also those in your Church, your community, this country, and this world., in this world. It must start somewhere, why not with us...This book was written by a group of women who are single, married, divorced, widowed, young, old, and most importantly, chosen just like you.

Virtuous Woman of God

May the Lord Jesus Christ bless you and anoint you as He has anointed women who have gone before you.

Be Blessed
with the patience of Sarah, who learned through trial and testing to submit to God's plan and His authority.

Be Blessed
with the balance of Martha's heart of servanthood and the heart of genuine love and worship shown by Mary.

Be Blessed
with joy, just as Mary, the mother of Jesus, joyfully received God's word, as well as her high calling to be a mother for our Savior.

Be Blessed
with the faith of Lois and Eunice, who willingly raised the young child Timothy, with the word of God. They knew the importance of preparing the next generation to serve Jesus.

Be Blessed
child of God and know that the Lord sees you as a beautiful white rose. May you grow in knowledge and wisdom as you gracefully blossom into the character of a Proverbs 31 woman. Jesus gave His life for you. Walk in His righteousness and the unfailing love of your eternal Father.

Figure 1 heartbeatofgod.org

Introduction

Contents

INTRODUCTION 3
By Robin Sykes

BIBLICAL WOMANHOOD 7

THE ATTACK ON WOMANHOOD 11

RESTORING WOMANHOOD 15

    SPIRITUAL HEALTH 19
    By Khalilah Cole

    EMOTIONAL HEALTH 23
    By Rosemary Devers

    MENTAL HEALTH 31
    By Patricia Jefferson

    NUTRITIONAL HEALTH 43
    By Lonna (Grandma Swann)

    PHYSICAL HEALTH 55
    By Evelisse Curbelo

THE CONCLUSION ON THE MATTER 67

ABOUT VIRTUOUS BY DESIGN 73

Each section has a place where you can take notes, journal, draw pictures, or mind maps. Use the space to document your healing, deliverance, and alter of remembrance of what God has done for you.

The Table of Contents

BIBLICAL WOMANHOOD

As a mother of six children ages ranging from 2 to 26, and being on my second marriage, I get it; you don't want to read another book telling you where you are missing it and that you can't obtain it. Well, this is not that book so read on...lol. **This book is for single and married women**. As a single woman, you still have womanhood priorities that call for you to be led by Christ, submitted to Christ, and in service to be used by Christ.

You were born with a purpose and called to a purpose. As you grow and go through the stages of womanhood, you may not know the purpose you were called to complete for the kingdom of God, but your purpose for being created was to be a woman in all her glory and fullness.

In Genesis 1:26 you will read that God created mankind. It did not say that he made man and then thought about making women. God already had a plan before creation started to make a woman; you are not an afterthought. He made a mate for every living creature; did you really think that he hadn't thought about a mate for Adam?

Then he gave us purpose. In Genesis 2:15 God gives man authority (headship) to rule over everything in the sea, the air, and on the earth. As you can see in Genesis 2:18 that women are included in that authority as a helper (suitable to him). Adam names Eve to also show that he is responsible for her and his headship over her confirming her dignity and worth. In this we learn that we are need of a covering for protection, provision, and to demonstrate personification of Christ and the Church or the image of God. God made woman, to be a suitable helpmate for the man He chose for her, to work in the earth and keep everything in its place.

For a woman to be a suitable helpmeet to her Adam, she needs to understand and embrace her womanhood, be whole, and walking in her calling. **As a suitable helpmeet:**
- You respond to his initiations for the service to the Lord.
- You surrender your name, your destiny, your will, your body, and your life to your children.
- You receive the given and do not insist in the not given (as Eve did).
- You submit your understanding, knowledge, opinions, feelings, and energies for the disposal of the person in authority over you.
- You are connected to your femininity and vulnerability.

It takes a separation from worldly thinking into Biblical thinking. A helpmeet can be bold, strong, and full of life and laughter while at the same time possessing a gentle quiet spirit that is submissive and respectful to others. Our femininity has nothing to do with our hobbies, interests, or colors that we like. Femininity is our ability to be relational, nurturing, vulnerable, beautiful from the inside, and responsive.

Now, if a man is a Cain instead of an Adam, this does not apply. Godless men have no authority and are ineligible to lead others. A woman married to an unbeliever should live her life submitted unto God**(1Peter3:1-2)**: Wives, in the same way submit yourselves to your own husbands so that, if any of them do not believe the word, they may be won over without words by the behavior of their wives, ² when they see the purity and reverence of your lives You are to follow the Biblical guidelines. **For the unmarried (2 Corinthians 6:14)**: Do not be unequally yoked with unbelievers. For what partnership has righteousness with lawlessness? Or what fellowship has light with darkness? For wives with unbelieving husbands. Make sure you choose someone who understands how to hear God's voice, submit to Him, and do His will.

Many of us have operated so long apart from our womanhood that we have forgotten why we are here and who we are here for. We can trace back the start of this separation from womanhood and manhood back to when Adam and Eve fell into sin. In Genesis 3:16 The woman is cursed with painful childbearing and having her husband rule over her though she will greatly desire him. This curse is hard for women today to even bare. We see women rejecting the natural nature to have and nurture children or marry men that they are a suitable helpmeet for, to marry men who they can rule over or even other women. In Genesis 3:17 we see the man receiving a curse for "listening to the woman". As women, we always wondered why it seemed like our husbands never listens to us…well now you know. Continue along this journey to discover how to get completely connected to your womanhood.

What do you need to confront in your own life that is opposing to Biblical womanhood? If you are not married, make a list of what your "Adam" that you are suitable for will possess? If you are married, what steps do you need to take to be a suitable helpmeet?

(Be creative, if drawing is better for you, use these spaces in whichever way you need to)

THE ATTACK ON WOMANHOOD

The original nature of womanhood, before sin, was to be relational, nurturing, vulnerable, beautiful from the inside out, and responsive. Once cursed with painful childbirth and a desire for a husband but having him rule over us; it caused many to separate from femininity which is womanhood. Not only that, the Bible has been used to "keep us in our place" and send us messages like, be Mary instead of Martha sitting at Jesus' feet and at the same time to be like a virtuous woman who wakes early and goes to bed late, whose day is filled with tasks that makes even the reader tired from reading all of the things she does. It is like a life of perfection that we know we will fall short on but exhaust ourselves trying to measure up. We invent our own definitions of femininity and design our own roles to establish our self-worth forgetting that our worth was created at the naming of Eve. No one ever tells us that it takes a balance between Martha and Mary to be in perfect harmony.

A new breed of women has stepped on the scene who are independent, in charge, and stressed out. Some who are even desiring the company of another woman which should not be. They are growing old early, having strokes and heart disease, normally do not have children but if they do are undisciplined, bitter because they are overlooked by suitable men, and are blaming everyone else for the state that they are in. See when a woman fails to see her mistakes, she is not only doomed to repeat them, but also has a hard time ever trusting or being in a loving relationship with an Adam. Have you ever noticed how some women cut their hair off after a breakup? It is directly related to her covering and the protection from a man that she is saying she no longer needs. Some of us will wait until we are broken, too old, or unattractive to decide that we are ready for our "Adam".

A woman can absolutely do what a man does, but why would she want too. A woman can be worldly successfully in leading a business, a ministry, her family, but she will never be satisfied. Everything that a leader is called to do goes against our Biblical nature causing a fight within ourselves that we will never win. A helpmeet that is suitable is one whose understanding, knowledge, opinions, feelings, and energies will supersede her "Adam" because she needs to be able to multitask and see the things her "Adam" can't see. She needs to be his herald running with the vision God gave him so that it can come to pass. This is why it seems that women have special powers. It was not given so that we can show them how much more powerful we are, or that we do not need them. We were created not because we needed them, but because God knew they needed us. We were created for the man and not the man for the woman. **So please stop saying you don't need a man, you are not supposed to.**

At some point in our lives it is like an evil clone of ourselves snatched us up and locked us away, and then presented itself to the world as if it was "us". After a while, we forgot who we were and slowly converted into that perverted image so by the time we escape, our identity is lost. The image of God that we once portrayed has now been distorted. See, the image of God is properly reflected when headship and submission are enacted within loving, equal, complementary male-female roles. When we flip the script and take on the male role, we call God a liar and become in the image of his adversary the devil. We ruin our home lives by tearing down our homes, Churches, and communities even though we may be worldly successful leaders. We will either lead our man to the true and living God Jesus or we can lead him to worship false Gods.

I am a woman of two marriages. My first season of being married, I was in constant battle for headship. I was a woman who knew what she wanted, and no one was going to stop me. I went to school to become an Engineer and then graduated and started making a six-figure income. I was the boss at work and wanted to be the boos at home. I thought my husband was weak in the area of leadership and did not know what was best for me and our two children, so I challenged him constantly. He was very physically and verbally abusive, but it was the way that he learned growing up to fight back. He did not know how to communicate or explain to me what I was doing wrong. He just knew that it was wrong. In spite the fact that he was not a Godly man and a tyrant, I was still wrong. So, what if he wasn't a great leader, my strengths could have lifted him up in front of the children and my softness could have turned away wrath. However, I was neither soft nor gentle; I was not humble or patient. I let my anger have its way and my discontentment have its full desire.

After the first marriage and a couple of relationships after, I learned of my cycle. I fell in love with a guy, and for the first time in my life, he decided that he did not love me back. It was the first time that I had actually given my heart and became vulnerable to a man and the first time that a man had broken it off with me. I was internally destroyed and mentally confused. God used the relationship to show me my heart, the things that were locked away and kept hidden even from me. The things that I was afraid to see about myself. I was a liar, I was a deceiver, I was a controller, and I was selfish in ways that I could have never imagine. Until that happened, I would just run when things were not easy or to my satisfaction. This time, everyone around me was pushing me away. It was then that I noticed that the clone of me was gone and I was becoming free. I ran to the feet of Jesus for my healing and deliverance. I became whole and then God brought me my husband after God's own heart; my Adam. You will have to read my book, In my Own Shadow, for the complete story ☺. What I learned though is that you can only realize your womanhood when you are functioning according to your created nature.

You should be a woman according to God's word for your ultimate good. "In six days, God gave man everything we needed to survive. Therefore, after sin, everything that was created came from our sinful desires or wants. After being exposed to good and evil, our desires were not always God's desires. So, everything that is now created is not necessarily what God wants for us to have. In many ways, we exchanged His perfect design for our own selfish desires." (Pastor Freddie Cole)

To purposefully not embrace our own gender outwardly is dishonoring to God. Some do it based on fear because their vulnerability was used against them. They operate out of the curse of Eve and fill their lives with worry, anxiety, and walls. Abuse, rejection, insult, and abandonment are common companions of loss of womanhood leaving a façade of holiness to avoid feeling vulnerable or to mask laziness.

We can get back to Eden, but first we have to admit that there is a need to return.

What are some of the ways that you realize you have not been operating in God's design for womanhood?

RESTORING WOMANHOOD

Truly feminine women receive, feel, express feelings in healthy ways, have strength in weakness versus a facade of strength. They experience hurt and trauma, but overcome trials and tribulations still being gentle and not bitter. Instead of keeping the bad things walled in, such as, defensiveness, promiscuity, false masculinity, operating in curses, detachment from others, avoidance behaviors, manipulation, control, depression, witchcraft, occultic participation, demonic defilement; she keeps the good. She is whole and healthy in all areas of her life:

- Spiritual health
- Emotional health
- Mental health
- Nutritional Health
- Physical Health

Your body is a temple of the Holy Spirit (1 Corinthians 6:19). The tabernacle and the Temple in Jerusalem had three parts: The outer court, the Holy Place, and the Holy of Holies. The presence of God dwelt solely in the Holy of Holies. Jesus found defilement in the outer courts with the money changers. It was where Jesus began to cast out defilement. Defilement is not found in the spirit of a Christian where the Holy Spirit resides "the Holy of holies" but in the "outer court" of the mind, emotions, and body. We are three-part beings: spirit, mind and emotions, and body. God wants His temple cleaned and every defiling demon cast out.

The first step would be for you to accept Jesus into your heart by believing that He died for your sins and is the resurrected son of God (the Christ), turn from your wicked ways, and go and sin no more. The next step is to be cleansed from the residue of the defilement which brings in healing and deliverance, and then have the house filled with Jesus by evidence of the fruit of the Spirit. The freer we become individually, the more able we are to help others. Our perfection in Christ is an ongoing process (Philippians 1:6).

The second step would be to cleanse the temple of defilement. The temple must be rid of demons because they oppose the things of the Spirit. Which means they are against the gifts of the Spirit because they counter the work of the demons. The gifts represent power and the fruit purity in which neither are present if the place is defiled. If the demons are present, you will never be able to live out your purpose or your calling.

The third step would be to fill the temple once cleared. The demons will be looking for a place that they can rest that is dry and waterless. After deliverance, the place will be left empty, swept, and unoccupied. You will need to fill the place with Jesus who has a never-ending supply of water by:

1. Staying connected with Jesus by being in fellowship with other believers and reading His Word. It is the Word that transforms. This will allow the life of Christ (The Holy Spirit) to flow into the branches (mind, will, and emotions) and produce fruit. The fruit of the Spirit are: Love, joy, peace, long suffering/Patience, Kindness, Goodness/Moral Purity, Faithfulness/ Loyalty, Meekness/ Gentleness, and Temperance/Self-Control. **The fruit of the spirit can't**

be produced by personal effort, it only comes by abiding in the vine!
2. Forgiving God, yourself, and others continually
3. Taking captive your thoughts so that you can have the mind of Christ. You don't want to have a crisis in your mind that is not based on reality.
4. Having faith and trusting God's love and protection.
5. Praying, petitioning, and giving thanks

<u>The fourth step</u> is to maintain the deliverance by putting on the whole armor of God, replacing negative thought patterns with positive ones, reading scripture continuously, crucifying the flesh, developing a life of praise, prayer, and worship, maintaining a life of fellowship and spiritual ministry, and committing yourself totally to Christ.

<u>The fifth and final step</u> would be to take authority over everything that creepth on the earth, flies in the air, and occupies the sea. We have to take authority over our minds, our households...etc.

Now it is time to dive into each element of womanhood to see how the human spirit can be confused with the demonic spirit. The devil wants to rule your mind, will, and emotions. It is time to learn his names, tactics, and schemes, and kick him out.

(Be humble before the Lord and let Him know everything that is troubling your heart or that was revealed to you from this section. Be creative, if drawing is better for you, use these spaces in whichever way you need to)

SPIRITUAL HEALTH
Deliverance, Authority, and Abiding
By
Khalilah Cole, DMin, MA, BS

Up until now, you have read the revelations giving to me about Biblical womanhood, the attack on womanhood, restoring womanhood, and now spiritual health. My journey with the Lord started at the age of five. Raised by a single mother, and being the youngest of four children, I had a lot of time to explore. As a child, my mother would read from the Bible and the Quran to us, she would listen to preachers on the radio and always speak of this wonderful Jesus who is there to help in times of trouble. Why did she need to do this; because trouble was everywhere. We lived in Bronx, New York then Oakland, California and finally Detroit, Michigan. These places were where the low income could come and thrive. When I say thrive, I mean pretend like they had more than their neighbors when inevitably they were just as poor. It was where crime would happen almost daily, and murder would be just around the corner. It is where I learned to steal, lie, and cheat to get what I wanted. It was where I learned that to be molested at five could have catastrophic consequences in your future that tells you it's okay for people to mis handle you sexually and to not tell.

On one side, I had a woman in the neighborhood that would take me to different churches to sing every week. On the other side, me and my siblings were going to malls and stores to take what we wanted. It was during a time where you could turn in cans and bottles for a refund, so that was our job in order to purchase food and buy the things we wanted. In this madness, I knew that I needed Jesus and so I accepted him into my heart, but it did not change me in an instant.

    As I grew from the age of five, I stopped stealing because of the only whooping my mother had given me for stealing a bike out of the shopping store and being brought home by the police. It was the first, and the misguided sexual acts was the second. The only issue is natural punishment cannot rebuke sexual sins. Sexual sins were sins of the flesh...sins that are tied to it which causes a tearing away to separate. It was not easy to pull apart from my natural identity. I went through years of self-hurt, people hurt, Church hurt, hurt that I can't even name, but then there were also years of me hurting and wounding others. I learned that God formed me perfectly but the selfish desires of man including my own caused a separation in my identity. I was lost but didn't even know it.

    God was slowly forming my inner beauty, while I was left physically unattractive to the world. I was a skinny lanky looking thing that was completely destroying my hair with dyes, perms, relaxers; whatever I would get my hands on to look like everyone else. I wanted to gain weight. I wanted to be accepted. I wanted friends. Moving from place to place year after year had always made me an outcast socially. Looking back, I realize that God was teaching me about inner beauty even then. I remained kind. I remained gentle. I remained loving. However, the more I tried to look like the world, the more I began to act like the world. I became more and more physically attractive and less and less beautiful on the inside. I started to allow the pain of what others were and had did to me to seep into my heart. Although I did not know that it was hurting me or contaminating me. I thought I was strong. That those things didn't bother me, but it was a mask of the enemy to keep me hurt instead of healed.

We can be believers but waste our energy and resources on the wrong things and never reach our full potential. For example, we can meditate on the wrong thoughts, beat ourselves up over past sins, or constantly compare ourselves to others. It keeps us from being delivered, abiding in Christ, producing good fruit, and taking authority so we are left powerless when we are supposed to be powerful, difference making, and victorious Christians.

My life needed to be pruned. I was a saved Christian living like I had no power, no self-control, fornicating, being used, and abused. I was being convicted but the soul ties had me bound by my hands and feet and so I couldn't walk away. I gave up my free will and asked God to intervene in my life. Once the man, that I decided to be vulnerable with and give my heart, left me, and all those around me left, I had nowhere to run but to Jesus. He patched me up, cut the strings of the bondage, and set me free. It all started with me giving Him permission to do so. I had to come out of agreement with the way I was living and the things that didn't "seem so bad" and come into agreement with His perfect will for my life.

The pruning process involved the renewing of my mind, focusing on Christ alone, training myself to seek Him daily in prayer, and reading His Word. It involved me getting into a healthy Church and fellowshipping with other believers. It caused me to turn my back on what I thought was me to become who I was meant to be. I had to get attached to the vine. Jesus is the vine. God the Father is the gardener. The fruits produced by the vine are the result of the inward working of the Holy Spirit and we as believers are the branches. It's a clear picture of all the roles at play. The gardener, God the Father, plants believers all over the world (John 15:1).

We must connect to Jesus by inviting His Spirit to come into our lives, save us from our sins, and bring us new life in Christ. When we have never experienced new life in Christ, we are spiritually dead, having no connection to the true source of life. Just like dead, brittle, dry branches, we have no potential for growth or life in us. This is why he prunes areas of our lives that are unproductive and weigh us down in our spiritual walk. For example, if there's an area that continually causes you to stumble, God will cut that branch off to free you in that area if you have given Him the authority to do so. He has our freedom in mind. As we do life with Jesus, He'll cast off areas in our lives that are better used for firewood.

What areas in your life need to be pruned?

EMOTIONAL HEALTH
Love in All the Wrong Places
by
Rosemary Devers

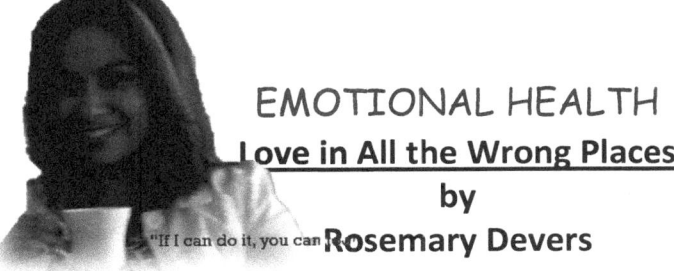

In Psalms 147:3 NKJV says He (The Lord) heals the brokenhearted and binds up their wounds. My Lord I pray that as I write that you illuminate my mind, my thoughts, and filter anything that is not of you, let your spirit be the one that speaks through the words that have been written in this section of this book, I pray that it blesses you, as it blessed me, as you read what the Lord has to say.

Emotional health is something that we as women need to understand and get a grasp on. Without having your emotions balanced it is hard to obtain or fill your full potential in the Lord. God has called us women to fulfill our ultimate purpose in him, whether it is at home, at work, in our careers, with our children, in ministry, or as wives.

As a young woman I dealt with insecurity issues. You see, I didn't grow up in the church like many, I grew up in South America. I was born in Lima, Peru. I went through hard times, because it was like living in a third world country. My mother raised us while my dad was mostly absent from the house due to work. His demanding job required him to be away a lot like a week or two at a time. I always felt like I needed to work hard to get my father's attention but never really had it. Something I always had to deal with. I really didn't feel accepted and loved by him. My mother dealt with insecurities since she was young, always searching for the acceptance and love of her parents but being the oldest of nine children it was nearly impossible. She carried that hurt and pain into her marriage with my dad. I always felt her frustration, I felt her unfulfillment, bitterness, sadness, depression; she was the one that raised me and my brother. My parents only wanted a small family. My father came from a large family as well, and was kind of in the middle, he is a twin. There were a total of ten brothers and sisters, you may say…" my goodness, no tv, at those times". Those times were different than ours. A lot of people had many children but the downfall to that is that the mothers were raising all the children at home and many were frustrated at times.

    I wanted to give you a little of my background because sometimes it's important to go back in the past to be able to understand and make adjustments per say for the future, and the breaking of chains that have been part of our lives. The things that keep us stuck and unable to fulfill our purpose.

    Well moving forward, when I was young, I always wanted to have my father's love, but didn't feel like I had it, always seeking approval from him. I hardly saw him in those years. I was going to school and helping my mother at home, my brother was small then. I saw my mother's frustration when I was young, my father was hardly there because of work, my father had many issues and one of them was that he loved to party with coworkers and drink a lot. So yeah, he was an absent parent; no wonder I felt the way as I did when I was young. One day my mother sent me to get groceries. She used to send me a lot to get water in buckets and groceries from the market. I was attacked by a mentally ill woman at the park that hit my head. On another occasion, I was touched inappropriately by a group of man on a corner as I was coming back from the store. I was about ten years old around that time. I never told my parents about that episode, but I did tell mom about what the crazy lady did, because I was traumatized. I didn't say anything of the other because I felt embarrassed about it. I used to hate going to the store by myself, I felt unprotected, and alone.

When I turned 15, an opportunity came along to come the US on a visa, my grandmother petitioned my father and his family, and my parents decided to take on that opportunity for the family. We came to the US in 1991, I was fifteen years old then and my brother was seven. We lived with my grandmother and aunt and her family. My father soon after found a job and so did my mother. My mother never worked but this time she had to, because starting over is very hard when you are an immigrant from another country. We didn't know a word of English. My brother and I were enrolled in school; I was enrolled in high school and my brother in elementary.

 Transitioning to me was very difficult; not knowing the language while also trying to fit in between girls my age. I was put in a class to learn English, and classes that I needed to graduate which were very hard on me because how did not know English. I did not know what was being spoken or even how to write. I graduated after a year later. I decided to go to college. At that time, I really didn't know what I wanted to be, I did it because my parents told me to. I was still struggling with the language and feeling uninspired, so I quit school and started working while living with my parents.

 My parents were very protective of me those years. They never let me go out with friends or go out to the clubs or anything like that. They used to say that because I was a woman, I could get assaulted and even murdered out there. In my head I thought about how is it now that you want to protect me, but when I needed the protection you were not there. I bought a car and met some friends and decided to move out; at that time, I was 21. I met a guy at work who I thought loved me. We went out a few times and lost my virginity to him in my car. Of course, it felt weird after that day, he never approached me, he got involved with another coworker later and I moved on. I made friends at work and we decided to live together; it was another girl. She had her room and I had mine. We would party together, smoked weed, get involved with some guys we would meet at the club. We were promiscuous, partying, and smoking weed. As young women we didn't really grasp the concept of self-worth. We believed anything anyone told us, and we didn't believe in ourselves.

      A couple of months after that I met a man, who was ten years older than me, through one of our group of friends. He would shower me with compliments on how beautiful I was, and he would buy me gifts and take me out eat. He wanted to be more than friends, so I let him in life. He was educated and I felt like a princess. **Ladies be careful of the counterfeits that maybe look like the one and is not.** After so many months things slowed down at work and I was forced to go back to my parents, so I kept seeing him. However, my parents were not very fond of him. They felt that he was hiding something.

      I became pregnant and when I told him, he said he would never get married because of a child. I felt devastated! I continued with that relationship even while I was hurt. He would lie to me and cheat on me even after having his child. He lived about forty-five minutes away, so we didn't see each other as often. This caused me to suffer because I always thought he was cheating, and he was. My mother helped raise my son. If it wasn't for the support of my family, I don't know what I would have done. The father of my son was not really coming to see him, he wasn't trying to be his father. I broke up with him many times, but I always found a way to forgive him and go back to the same cycle I knew. He would always promise my son that he was sending gifts in the mail and my son was always heartbroken when it wasn't true. I finally found courage to end it, I told him I was done, and I couldn't take his lies, cheating, broken promises to my son. I knew the only way to be sure was cut it from the root. I changed my number, changed my email account, so he wouldn't contact me. He moved to another state, so to me it was a relief that he was not going to be around me so it wouldn't have the temptation to go back. I worked hard, but one thing I promised myself was that I would never have another child until I was in an established relationship and married. I didn't want another child of mine to go through what my son had to go through. It was on me to make these changes in my life. **When you are trying to heal from deep hurts, the best medicine a lot of times is distance, time and patience.**

    I was introduced to the Lord a year or so later through a common friend. I didn't really understand how I was supposed to have a relationship with Jesus. I listened to what had been preached, but couldn't really grasp the importance, so kept seeking in different places for someone to love me. I would try internet dating; met a few men there, but to me it was more for the attention I was getting. **I feel today that what I was looking for is exactly what I didn't get while I was young; that is love and attention from my father, the first man in my life.**

    I met my husband online, but it was different I wasn't looking this time around. He searched for me. Although he seemed nice, I had my guard up. I wanted to be friends first and so we did. He was from another state and we talked every day, he was a practicing minister in his father's church and that encouraged me. I was done with all the counterfeits and I was ready for the real deal, so I gave it a chance and this time trusted the Lord to guide me. I prayed that he was a real man of God and not another counterfeit, and long and behold we got married. In marriage, everything is not easy because we are two different people trying to make things work. However, with God being the lead in our lives, there is comfort and peace.

As I reflect on these situations, I allowed myself to go through, I realized a lot of it was me not understanding where my heart was. Healing was not taking place, I was looking for love and acceptance in all the wrong places, I was playing in the devil's playground, leaving emptiness, unfulfillment, resentment, and bitterness. If I would have recognized the trap of the enemy at any of those different times, I would have stopped cycle from continuing.

When I take a look at now, I have strong relationship with the Lord. I know Him to be my deliverer of my pain. I know he thinks of me with so much love, telling me I am his daughter, a jewel, his pride, his pearl. While looking for love in the wrong places, I realize I am his and He has been there all along. He is my father, my identity lies in him, I am His creation, what is more precious than that. In Him I learned the true definition of love as listed in the chart below. It is the **agape love that remains forever**. The kind of love that my husband shows me. What my child's father and the others gave me was the **eros (lust) kind of love** that will never remain and is insatiable, never satisfied and seeking to please self. I would receive the **philos kind of love from my family and friends**, but I needed the love from my father like the love that my Father in heaven showers down on me.

Ladies lastly love yourselves. We have a purpose, we are loved by the almighty God and He should be our first love not the last. He can break chains of bondage; he can stop the enemy on his tracks. Position yourselves with your maker.

Don't sell yourself short to just anyone, you are precious. Above all else, guard your heart until your "Adam" finds you. If you guard your heart, you will choose wisely and disregard the counterfeits without causing damage to your heart. A broken is hard to mend and may have you bringing broken pieces to the husband God has waiting for you. Believe me when I say, if you keep following the same path, the outcome will never change.

Word	Meaning	Comments	Biblical Usage
Agapē (Gk.)	Indicates a choice to serve God, to love neighbor, to accept self without expecting something in return (Matt. 22:34–40).	Appears rarely in secular Greek writings; Coined by New Testament writers to describe God's love (John 3:16); Christian love is based on the deliberate choice of the lover rather than the worthiness of the one loved (1 Cor. 13:1–13).	Love: is longsuffering is kind is not jealous is not boastful is not arrogant is not rude is not selfish is not resentful does not think evil rejoices in truth bears all things believes all things hopes all things endures all things (1 Cor. 13:1–13).
Philos (Gk.)	Refers to esteem and affection reflected in the loving concern friends have for one another.	Used in the New Testament (John 21:15–17; Titus 2:4); Sometimes used interchangeably or synonymously with agape.	The nature of Peter's love is the question. Jesus uses agapē (unselfish commitment) in His questions; Peter uses philos (esteem or high regard) in his response. Perhaps his caution comes from his bitter experience of denying the Lord (John 21:15–17). The love of a woman for her husband and children must be marked with philos or esteem and respect, not just agapē or unselfish commitment (Titus 2:4; see also Eph. 5:33).
Eros (Gk.)	Describes appetitive, self-centered love, including sexual desire and physical craving.	Does not appear in the New Testament.	
Stergos (Gk.)	Alludes to affection, especially among family members.	Does not appear in the New Testament.	

Figure 2 Patterson, Dorothy; Kelley, *The Woman's Study Bible* (Thomas Nelson, 1995), p. 1918.

What changes do you need to make to change your current cycle to put you on the path that God has designed for you?

MENTAL HEALTH
God and Mental Health Awareness
By
Patricia L. Jefferson, MCPSS, MA, BA

Thank God I woke up in my right mind this morning. To wake up in my right mind takes prayer and a comfortable sleep. Trust in the Almighty God and his Son King Jesus' words have strengthened me. After years of distraction and seeking something, anything to fill emotional holes in my life, I have a new mind set.

After the death of my father and then my oldest daughter, I was diagnosed with Major Depression and Anxiety. During my recovery, I was educated by the State of Michigan in Mental Health and I was Certified as a Peer Support Specialist. I have assisted many in mental health recovery through support groups.

After the death of my husband Dwight L. Jefferson, Veteran, I fully experienced the Lenten Season Purification Ceremony, with the Shrine of the Black Madonna Orthodox Christian Church. The Purification Ceremony started early one "Sonday" morning. It began with me on my knees at the altar with my hands up in the air pleading for openness. When I returned to my seat the transformation had begun and I was ready to receive what was to come. The entire ceremony I was lifted mentally and emotionally. Physically, I sat there and trembled. I trembled through the washing of the hands in hyssop. I trembled right through the sermon. I received purification.

I was redeemed as a child of God, right then and there. God had forgiven me. I am forgiven of all hurts and injuries, mentally and physically. Received hurts and perpetrated hurts. I was free of all guilt, failures, shame, and regrets. I had surrendered, I am free!

Since my arrival here in Florida with my daughter and son in law; Pastors Freddie and Khalilah Cole, I am spiritually fed by their church, Grace Restoration. My new eyes have revealed, that faith does help in recovery. As it does in substance abuse programs every day.

The key awareness: God so loved you – he gave his son for you. King Jesus is the representative power of God's Love. Jesus is the body of love. This love is real it is presented to us in Jesus' own words. To trust in these words takes faith. Faith is like the wind; it cannot be seen but it is very powerful. Life in America requires power. It requires faith.

98% of all Americans experience some trauma in their lifetime. Trauma is a deeply disturbing experience. Psychological trauma is a type of damage to the mind that occurs as a result of a distressing event. Traumatic events injuries can be greater than the resilience of a person. An overwhelming amount of stress that exceeds one's ability to cope or to integrate the emotions involved with that experience. Trauma may result from a single distressing experience or reoccurring events of being overwhelmed that is experienced in weeks, years, or even decades. The person struggles to cope with the immediate circumstances, which can eventually lead to serious long-term negative consequences. Some, cope better that others with these challenges. 1 in every 25 adults in the U.S. experience a serious mental illness in a given year that substantially interferes with or limits major activities. 1 in 5 youth age 13-18 experiences a severe mental disorder at a point during their life. Mental Health healing is needed, thank God recovery is real.

Research has shown that verbalizing feelings about experiences can have a therapeutic effect on the brain. In other words, to speak about your feelings and concerns while believing that you are heard and managed is good for your wellbeing. Many trusts in the professionals that they share their feelings and concerns with. My point is, trust in God. God is a good listener.

One set of footprints instead of two on the sand, Jesus carried you. Recognize that power of survival! Trust in his word know Jesus is right there as a comfort. With God, Mental Health healing is emotional and behavioral. In faith your mind is stayed on Jesus. Your behavior is modified to live according to God's plan. Your purpose is a filled hole-less life. Keep the faith trust in God.

But straightaway Jesus spoke to them saying, be you of good cheer; it is I: Be Not Afraid. And Peter answered him and said, Lord if it be you, bid me come to you on the water. And Jesus said, Come. And when Peter was come down out of the ship, he walked on water to go to Jesus. But when Peter saw the wind boisterous, he was afraid; and as he began to sink, he cried saying, Lord, save me. And immediately Jesus stretched forth his hand, and said to him, O you of little faith, why did you doubt? Mat. 14:22-31

So, have no doubts and keep the faith. Faith comes by the hearing, and hearing by the words of God. Faith comes by hearing the words of Jesus, speak them. When you strengthen your faith; you will strengthen your courage. Study the bible, let the words of Jesus light your heart. Learn the words like you learned the alphabets, recite them. The words will prove to be a strong handhold during your daily life. Find a church home where bible use is the practice. Join the women or men group. Share your feelings and concerns while you support others in the meetings. Faith and trust in the word will become a lifestyle. Most of all know God is Love.

Retaining one's deliverance from mental illness requires breaking the habit of negativity in one's mind. Following deliverance, this is done by replacing negative thought patterns with positive ones and promises from the Word of God. Hence, we take captive every thought that stands in opposition to scripture. (2 Corinthians 10:5) We demolish arguments and every pretension that sets itself up against the knowledge of God, and we take captive every thought to make it obedient to Christ.

F alse
E vidence
A ppearing
R eal

False evidence, if believed, can have fatal results!
Seek Peace of Mind!
Patricia L. Jefferson, Stepping into Greatness

False evidence can lead to demonic infestations such as Schizophrenia also known as split personalities. Schizophrenia can be demonically inherited. It's in the demons, not the genes. Demons seek to perpetuate their like kind which is easier in families. When a mother is full of rejection, she is responsible for feeding love into the family. The rejection the mother is feeling is now fed to her children and husband in the way that she handles them. The child Is now open to the spirit of rejection. You can have a rejection spirit and still manage to form your own personality and be secure in yourself, but the schizophrenic will always be floundering asking "Who am I?" The identity of the true self will be confused or lost. In the illustrations that follow, the <u>left-hand shows rejection</u> as the control demon; it is agony within, a starvation of love, insecurity, inferiority, fantasy, unreality, etc. (Hammond, Frank; Hammond, Ida, 1973)

The right-hand shows rebellion as the control demon. When one does not have satisfactory love relationships when growing up, they are unable to feel and share in love relationships. A rebellion spirit sets in. They begin to fight for love or lash out at those who may have starved them of love. Rebellion asserts itself in stubbornness, self-will, and selfishness. This is another personality that can be identified by aggressiveness, lashing out, anger, bitterness, resentment, hatred, and retaliation. A schizophrenic can switch from one personality type to another in moments. Rebellion is the opposite of rejection. One is expressive and turbulent and the other is withdrawn and insecure. (Hammond, Frank; Hammond, Ida, 1973)

The real person is neither hand. The demons have not permitted the real person to develop, therefore the schizophrenic does not know the real self. When the schizophrenic person begins to be delivered, the real self must have Jesus. Jesus must start growing in the person, developing the personality, and making it what He wants it to be. This could take several months or even a year, or longer. It takes time because if every demon was to be cast out at once it would leave the schizophrenic person lost. When a schizophrenic person is put to the test of something like coming under submission, they will either fall back into rejection by fleeing; into rebellion by expressing anger, stubbornness, or defiance; or yield to authority by becoming cooperative falling out of agreement with the demons to break old habit patterns. The real self must become strong enough in Christ to carry through on the right choices. (Hammond, Frank; Hammond, Ida, 1973)

<u>The hurricane swirls</u> in the illustration between the hands represents the storms that the schizophrenic person continually creates. The storms or drama around themselves. The person is caught up in the storms. The storms with arrows are the storms brought in from others who are trying to relate but are unstable themselves causing storms within the storms. The arrows without storms are stable people who can relate to the hurricane in a stable way. This person can engage the storm without being damaged or scarred. He is not captured by the turmoil. The person ministering deliverance to the schizophrenic must be the stable arrow. These storms cause the root of bitterness to form (see the right hand) and to be driven deeper and deeper.

<u>From the false personality of rejection comes</u> lust or sensual love with a companion spirit of fantasy lust. Fantasy lust puts a person in the role of being a great lover in a film. This then leads to the harlotry spirit in women manifesting itself in provocative dress. Sexual perversions represent extreme attempts to overcome rejection. Sexual experiences, real or imaginary, can never satisfy the need for genuine love. It will have you riddled with frustration and guilt leading to insecurity and inferiority. It doesn't stop there, next is self-accusation that the demon uses to destroy your self-worth which sometimes leads the person into the compulsion to confess, but it is not repentance. The person generally confesses to those who show him the most love and is driven to shock others into giving him forced attention and find a substitute for love.

<u>From the false personality of rebellion comes</u> self-will which is attached to selfishness. This opens the way for stubbornness, unteachableness. Since the person has been rejected for years, he is driven to pamper self. Then comes

accusation which is a compensation spirit to draw attention away from the rejection. It takes the attention off of self to put it on others. The left finger points at self while the right finger points at others to blame which opens the door to judgmentalism. The next step then is self-deception which companions, delusion, self-seduction, and pride. One who feels rejection wants to feel important and so the spirit of delusion tells them that they are REALLY important. It only leads to greater frustration and disappointment. (Hammond, Frank; Hammond, Ida, 1973)

<u>The thumbs represent paranoia</u>, believing or seeing things that are not true and based on lies instead of reality. On the rejection side are jealousy and envy because those who are deficient in reciprocal love relationships become jealous and envious of those who do experience satisfying love. On the rebellion side are the spirits of distrust, suspicion, fears, and persecution, and the confrontation with honesty at all costs Suspicion and distrust build up in a person until they ae compelled to confront the other person. After confrontation dies down within the person, the pressure dies down for a while, but the confronted person is left to handle his wounds. The person acting under the influence of paranoid demons is quite insensitive as to how many wounds they cause yet they are super sensitive to every offense toward themselves. There is a root of bitterness. With life, conflict happens, and words are spoken that require an attitude of forgiveness. The problem with a schizophrenic person is that they are unable to forgive. They have an unforgiving spirit. The things that happened 10, 20, 30 years ago are still alive as if they happened a minute ago allowing the root of bitterness to form into resentment, hatred, anger, retaliation, violence, possibly murder, and many more.

The three main areas to conquer are rejection, rebellion, and the root of bitterness. For rebellion is as the sin of witchcraft, and stubbornness is as iniquity and idolatry (1 Samuel 15:23a)

I WILL BE DIFFERENT! I WILL NOT ALLOW DEMONS TO RULE MY LIFE!

Prayer for Deliverance

Lord Jesus Christ, I believe you died on the cross for my sins and rose again from the dead. You redeemed me by your blood, and I belong to you, and I want to live for you, I confess all my sins, known and unknown, sins of commission or omission, I am sorry for all of them. I renounce them all. I forgive all others as I want you to forgive me. Forgive me now and cleanse me with your blood. I thank you for the blood of Jesus Christ which cleanses me from all sin. I come to you now as my deliverer. You know my special needs, the thing that binds, torments, and defiles me; that evil spirit **(name them)**, that unclean spirit **(name them)**. Demons' I know that you are there. I know your presence and your evil works. I tell you that you have no right to stay. I belong to Jesus Christ. This body is the temple of the Holy Spirit. Everything that defiles it is cast out. You are a trespasser and you must go. I claim the promise of your word "whosoever that calleth on the Lord shall be delivered." I call upon you now. In the name of the Lord Jesus Christ, deliver me and set me free. Satan, I

renounce you and all your works. I loose myself from you in the name of Jesus, and I command you to leave me right now, I hold my conquered ground.
In Jesus' name. Amen!

Diagram this page with the things that Christ says you are; and with things that interest you. Let the real you show up on this page so that you will never forget again.

THE REAL SELF

Mental Health

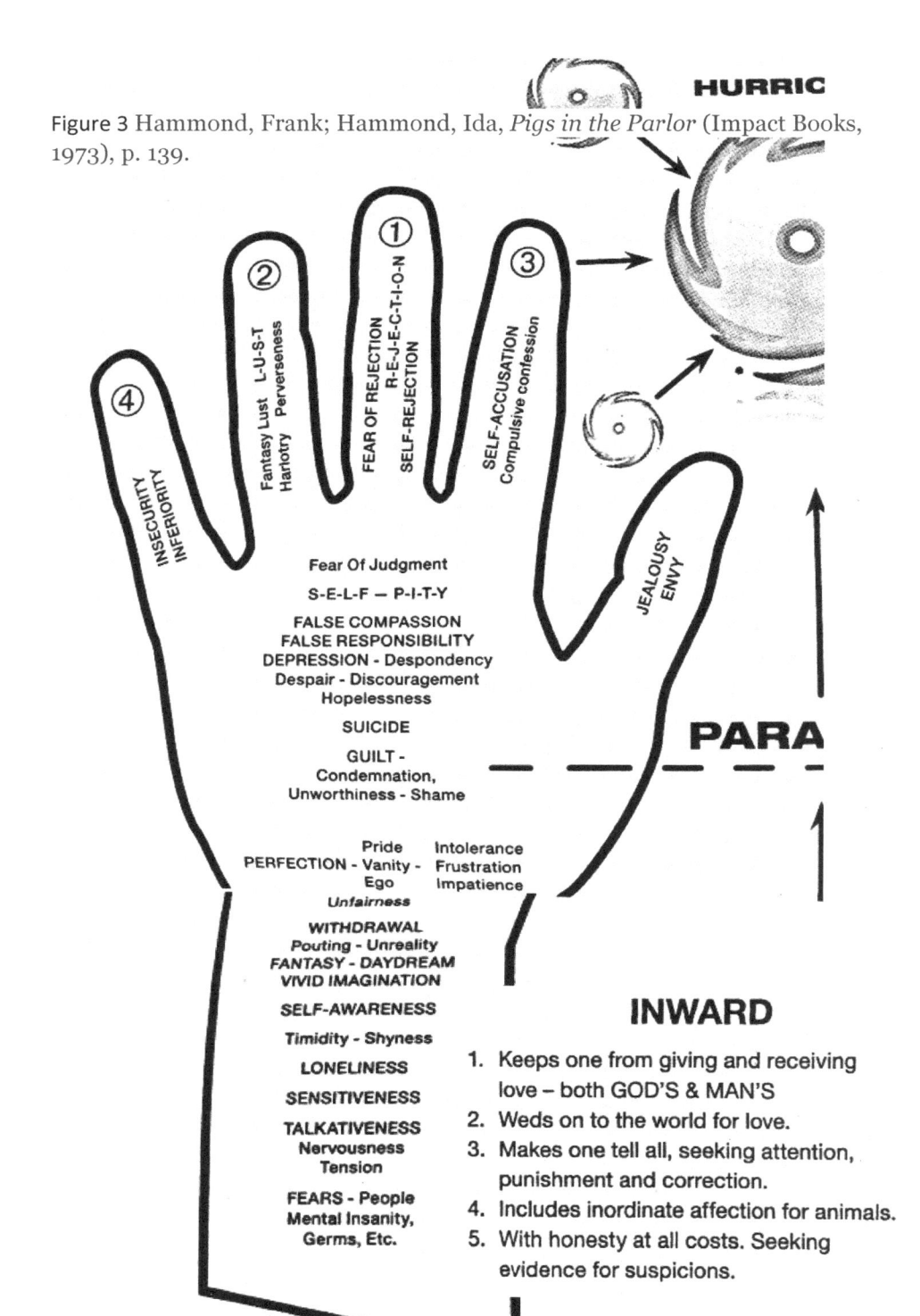

Figure 3 Hammond, Frank; Hammond, Ida, *Pigs in the Parlor* (Impact Books, 1973), p. 139.

HURRIC

① FEAR OF REJECTION
R-E-J-E-C-T-I-O-N
SELF-REJECTION

② L-U-S-T
Fantasy Lust   Perverseness
Harlotry

③ SELF-ACCUSATION
Compulsive confession

④ INSECURITY
INFERIORITY

JEALOUSY
ENVY

Fear Of Judgment
S-E-L-F — P-I-T-Y
FALSE COMPASSION
FALSE RESPONSIBILITY
DEPRESSION - Despondency
Despair - Discouragement
Hopelessness

SUICIDE

GUILT -
Condemnation,
Unworthiness - Shame

Pride   Intolerance
PERFECTION - Vanity -   Frustration
Ego   Impatience
Unfairness

WITHDRAWAL
Pouting - Unreality
FANTASY - **DAYDREAM**
VIVID IMAGINATION

SELF-AWARENESS
Timidity - Shyness

LONELINESS

SENSITIVENESS

TALKATIVENESS
Nervousness
Tension

FEARS - People
Mental Insanity,
Germs, Etc.

PARA

INWARD

1. Keeps one from giving and receiving love – both GOD'S & MAN'S
2. Weds on to the world for love.
3. Makes one tell all, seeking attention, punishment and correction.
4. Includes inordinate affection for animals.
5. With honesty at all costs. Seeking evidence for suspicions.

Mental Health

RRICANE

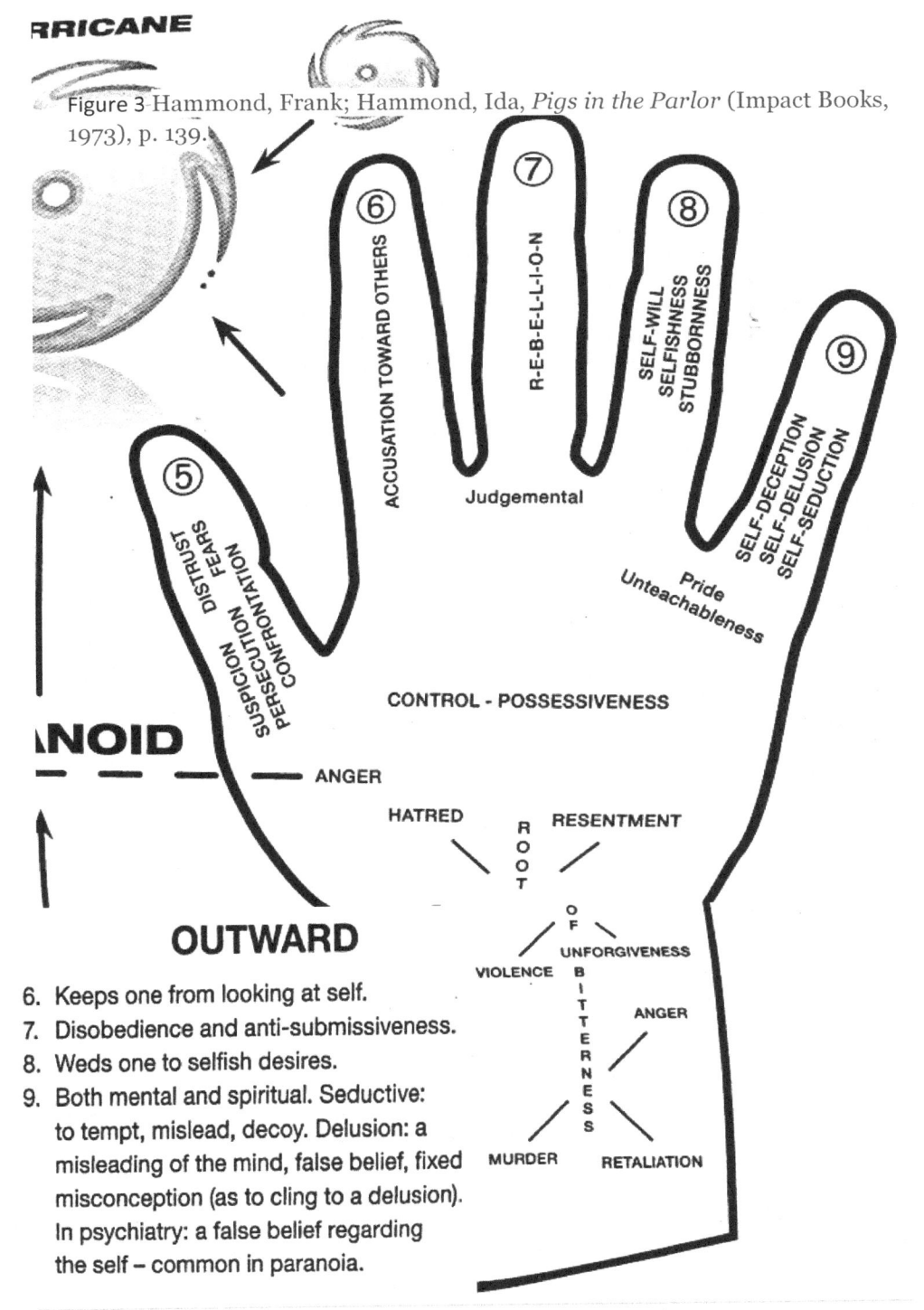

Figure 3 Hammond, Frank; Hammond, Ida, *Pigs in the Parlor* (Impact Books, 1973), p. 139.

⑥ ACCUSATION TOWARD OTHERS

⑦ R-E-B-E-L-L-I-O-N

⑧ SELF-WILL / SELFISHNESS / STUBBORNNESS

⑨ SELF-DECEPTION / SELF-DELUSION / SELF-SEDUCTION

⑤ DISTRUST / FEARS / SUSPICION / PERSECUTION / CONFRONTATION

Judgemental

Pride
Unteachableness

CONTROL - POSSESSIVENESS

ANOID

— ANGER

HATRED   R   RESENTMENT
          O
          O
          T

          O
          F

VIOLENCE   UNFORGIVENESS
          B
          I   ANGER
          T
          T
          E
          R
          N
          E
          S
MURDER   S   RETALIATION

OUTWARD

6. Keeps one from looking at self.
7. Disobedience and anti-submissiveness.
8. Weds one to selfish desires.
9. Both mental and spiritual. Seductive: to tempt, mislead, decoy. Delusion: a misleading of the mind, false belief, fixed misconception (as to cling to a delusion). In psychiatry: a false belief regarding the self – common in paranoia.

Mental Health

What strongholds do you need to break free from to fill your temple with the stronghold of Christ? Write and recite your prayer.

NUTRITIONAL HEALTH
My Health Passion
By
Lonna (Grandma) Swann

As Women of God, I believe we carry the greatest responsibility for our families and their health. Even if we are the "bread winners" we also usually have to be the "bread fixers or" bread providers" for our family. In this world and its systems that seem to be challenging us, at every turn, we may need to look to the simplicity of God's plan for the health of our bodies.

In the Beginning
God has a purpose for everything and everybody, and created everything we needed to sustain us, before he created man/woman:
1. God said it. (Established what was, in the mind of God).
2. God Made it (formed and made it visible and functional)
3. God Set a Plan in motion to sustained itself (multiply after his kind.) Gen 1
4. God created man/woman in His own image and likeness.
5. God gave them(us) dominion/authority over the fish of the sea, birds of the air, all the earth, everything on and around the earth and all creeping things. (all living things)
6. God gave us green plant bearing seed and tree bearing seed (self-sustaining) for our food.

Cells are the basic building blocks of all living things. The human body is composed of trillions of cells. They provide structure for the body, take in nutrients from food, convert those nutrients into energy, and carry out specialized functions.

- Our bodies were created by God.
- Our bodies were created for His purpose.
- We are spirit, we have a mind and we live in a body.

When our body dies, we live on, our real self continues on in eternity, one place or the other, depending on whether we receive what Jesus did for us or not.

When we believe, and confess with our mouth, and receive the Lord Jesus into our hearts (spirit), we are born a new, spiritual birth, and we are new creatures in Christ Jesus. (II Corn. 5:17)   Jesus then abides in us, works through us and he has redeemed us from the curse of the Law Deut:28, Gal.3:13, (Sickness, disease, poverty, etc…) by His stripes we were healed. (IPet.2:24)

> **Foot note:** You can stop reading right now, if you have not received Jesus into your heart, and you can receive Him right now by doing the above. The rest will not make sense to you, unless you have been born again.

Our bodies are what we live in, on this earth, which we have dominion and stewardship over (to dress it and keep it Gen 1; 2:15). We also have dominion/authority over the adversary. He can only do what we allow him to do. We need to be watchful that we don't give him a place to operate from, by opening a door to sickness and disease through our choice of what we feed our cells.

Adams & Eve (we) were given free will, to choose, and given dominion and authority over all the earth to be good stewards and use stewardship, wisely and responsibly. Adam and Eve were deceived out of their rights, but their sin (choice) allowed sin nature (sickness, disease, corruption and death) into the earth. There are consequences for every choice. We can choose the choice, but we cannot choose the consequences. We were given free will, and dominion and authority over all the earth. That did not change, we still have it. (Gen 1:28)

Our adversary and things on this earth only have the power and authority that we choose to give them. Get it? The "dominion" that plants have over us (Tobacco, Alcohol, Drugs, money. Sugar, etc...) are there because we chose it. Rather than taking dominion over them, we've allowed them to "rule" us.

We are to take responsibility and stewardship over the things God has given us to "rule". God gave us cells, we are responsible, we have to feed them what they eat. Pure potent and effective food.

How have we done, so far? We have ignored God's instructions and depleted the very soil that our "life" comes from. We've added chemicals, emulsifiers, dyes, artificial additives, preservatives. We have removed even the "germ" of the grains (which is the "life" of the plant, that has the most nutrition) and replaced it with synthetic vitamins and call it enriched. All in the name of taste good and look good.

The Plant Breeders, those that breed plants to produce "better" strains for plant production, have 7 goals for food production.

1. Yield per acre (Producing more food per acre meaning less nutrients per plant.
2. Resistance to insects (insecticides, GMO's etc..)
3. Drought tolerance
4. Ease of Mechanical Harvesting
5. Lengthy storage
6. Transports well. (they "create" hybrids to be hardier)
7. Appearance

Notice that none of the goals are <u>Nutritional value for people</u>. Greed would seem to be the dominant theme.

What about Cells?

Our body is made up of trillions of cells, (bone cells, blood cells, brain cells, organ cells, etc...) They were created by God, to absorb nutrients, fight disease and reproduce after his kind.

So, our Cells only eat (absorb, take in) FOOD (nutrients; vitamins, mineral, protein, Carbohydrates and fats) that's it! The body also needs an environment of clean water, clean air and exercise and rest, to function properly.

To protect the body, cells react to (or fight) anything that is not a food. (Medication, chemical additives, preservatives, pesticides & herbicides, artificial stuff, stress, etc...), you know, the stuff we feed our bodied. That is why every Prescription Medication has a side effect. It is also why Medication works, (if it does) because it is designed to cause a reaction.

The energy that it takes for cells to react, fight off, and process non-foods, deplete the nutrients meant for fighting disease and building health.

Cells also respond (react) to stress and environmental toxins, like, what we put on our skin, (60% of what we put on our skin is absorbed into our blood stream) what we breath (air pollution) and what we drink (our water supply is polluted).

One Disease

Therefore, there is only **one disease**. It is called **MALFUNCTION OF THE CELLS. There are two causes of Malfunction of the cells:**

Malnutrition: The body is not getting enough nutrients to supply the demand. Either not enough food (starvation), or the soil has been so depleted that the nutrients are not there anymore.

Toxins: The body is getting so much toxins material that it uses all the energy produced by healthy cells to fight their effects in the body. And/or the cells get so overwhelmed with "junk" that they cannot even absorb and process the nutrients meant to nourish the cells and thus, the body.

Our food supply is so polluted and depleted, that it is difficult for us to get the food (nutrients) we need to build and sustain health. That is why America is 36th in world health (below some third world countries) and #1 in health cost per capita. We are living longer, but also living sicker longer. That is why supplementation is necessary to fill in the gaps. Even if we eat organic, which is the best choice for food, we cannot be sure it is pure. Our ground water, acid rain, and drifting chemicals can wreak havoc on our organic choices.

OK, which kind of supplements?

Unfortunately, all food supplements are not created equal. If the Supplements you choose are **synthetics** (not food), your cells will react, much like they react to Prescription drugs and eventually they will deplete the body because they are not feeding it, your cells are reacting.

If you choose "natural" Supplements, they may be better (or not). The Food Supplement Industry is not well regulated, and a supplement can contain only 10% natural ingredients to be labeled "Natural" (refined sugar is considered natural). Also, deceptive labeling and use of poor-quality ingredients are an issue.

So, what do we do?

Above all, be sure to thank the Lord, ask Him to bless and sanctify your food before you consume it! However, knowingly eating poisons, or harmful, depleted foods, when we can do better, and asking the Lord to bless and sanctify it, seems to be a far cry from the wisdom and stewardship he has given us, and expects us to use.

Our bodies are the only "house" on this earth that we have to live in and is home to the Holy Spirit. How we respect and care for it, is important to God, because our purpose on this earth, in this body, deserves a healthy, functional body that will not distract us from God's intended purpose. Jesus healed us over 2,000 years ago and even though we receive our healing, maintaining it can be a daunting task in the world we live. There are a couple of solutions:

1. make great strides to live "organically", analyze everything we eat, avoid the Fast foods, avoid all preservatives, additives, and altered foods, grow and prepare all of our foods ourselves watch what we drink and attempt to circumvent the greed and profit driven worlds systems. That can be very time consuming and stressful.

2. The option I chose, is to trust God, and be conscious of my food choices and be diligent about not recklessly indulging in foods that are low in food value and filled with toxins. But I also have found the only Company that I know of, that has Food Supplements, that do clinical studies to prove their effectiveness and purity, and has integrity in their practices and manufacturing and is guaranteed to make you feel better in 30 days or your money back. Shaklee's goal is to make products as close to nature as possible, and the Company is based on the "Golden Rule". The Shaklee Corporation has existed for over 60 years, I have been consuming Shaklee products for 45 years. I am 76 years old, on no prescription medication and have no aches or pain, blood work is normal, blood pressure is normal, and I am in my right mind, lots of energy, good memory, accomplishing God's plan for my life, while full-time RV-ing and loving life.

When I was younger, low energy, allergies, arthritis, depression, colds & flu regularly, severe PMS issues, headaches, etc... My husband had low energy, and prostate problems. We were working for the government in Washington DC, tired of our jobs, living from payday to payday when Shaklee appeared in our lives in an unexpected way/

We were introduced to Shaklee in 1974 by my parents, **Orlin & Alma Lett** from Myrtle Point, Oregon; they were in their 60's. Orlin had retired due to heart problems; he had arthritis and was blind in one eye. Alma had allergies so bad that she had to take shots twice a week and still had runny nose and eyes most of the time as she was allergic to so many things and was over 144 lbs. overweight. Knowing their condition and the decline of people generally in that state, we paid for what we thought would be their last trip to see us in Maryland. We planned to discuss their burial plans during the month that they were to stay with us (that never happened).

Well, we didn't know that they had been using Shaklee Food Supplements for 6 months before they came and when they got off the plane, they looked better than we had ever remembered seeing them. They were up early, out late, out jogging and we couldn't keep up. Dad had an EKG before he came and there was no trace of heart problems, he had no problem with his arthritis, and he discovered while visiting with us that he could see out of the eye he had been blind in for 6 years. We were amazed and then we left my Mom's shots in the refrigerator at home when we went on a trip to New England and that was when she knew she didn't need her shots anymore.

They brought a suitcase full of Shaklee tapes that we listened to on the trip and we were pretty impressed, but cautious. We called the Better Business Bureau and their report stated that there were no consumer complaints on file for Shaklee. We had been looking for a business and after we saw the results that Lonna's parents received with the products, we tried them ourselves and got results, Shaklee was it for us. **Howard Larew** flew out from California our third day in Shaklee and set up our One on One presentation book and did our first meeting with **James and Veronica Coates**, and two others attending. Three months later we were Sales Leaders and I have enjoyed 45 years of sharing the Shaklee good news and enjoying the benefits.

Orlin and Alma got excited before they left, went back to California where they had been looking for a Rest Home. They spent a month going to every meeting they could find, filled a U-Haul full of Shaklee product (you needed to stock products

Nutritional Health

back then) and went back to Oregon to build their Shaklee business. Three months later, the Lett's became Sales Leaders and for the next twenty-five years they took no medication, Alma lost 144lbs and kept it off, they earned 11 Bonus Cars and went on every all-expense paid trips Shaklee offered together with us, having a great luxurious time all over the world. What a life!

Alma went home to Jesus at age 88, and Orlin at age 96, enjoying a great life in their right mind, and making a difference in thousands of lives, what a legacy!

We started our Shaklee with a lot of excitement and enthusiasm and attracted a lot of people who wanted to feel better and live a better lifestyle. We resigned our "Good government jobs" and were full-time Shaklee, our second year. Sharing better health and financial freedom with others, earned us 11 bonus cars and free travel every year, to some exotic destination in the world. I have earned income of a minimum of $2000 every month for 45 years from our Shaklee Business and have been honored on stage at the last 5 Shaklee Conventions as having earned over a Million dollars from our Shaklee business. That includes two 6-year periods where we did nothing to grow our business and our income did not diminish.

My Husband. Floyd, became a Minister and finished his course, going home to be with the Lord in June of 2012, after making a huge impact that has and will remain. We were happily married for 43 years, and when I realized, that he was enjoying Jesus and was probably not thinking about me, and if I was to grieve and stop my life, I would be (selfishly) thinking about me, and I would not finish what God purposed for me to do. I may have time to grieve later, but I must fulfill the purpose God has for me first.

I had a stroke in 2014 (with no residual symptoms remaining), pre-cancerous lesions on my intestines, (no longer there), my bone density has increased by 5.9%. I had a liver cyst that was as large as a melon which burst and was surgically removed in 2017 (that is when I found out I was in perfect health, Praise the Lord). It is like a water balloon in my liver, made from liver tissue, and it grew back last year. It doesn't bother me, so I'm not bothering it, it will be gone soon. Praise God! My Doctor said if it becomes a problem, I will know it. It is healed!

I like simplicity. Confusion and chaos are not of God. I found Shaklee to be simple and based on Godly principles. Shaklee has a health assessment (called HealthPrint) that, based on completing a questionnaire, which takes about 5 minutes, gives suggestions on how to improve your health (with your budget in mind). The suggested products are guaranteed to bring you better health in 30 days, no matter how good or bad you feel, even returning the empty container.

There was a 6-year period where we left off doing our Shaklee business, when my husband entered the Ministry. Shaklee had become so exciting almost a "god" in our lives. We had to be willing to let it go, even though it was our only source of income. Well, we couldn't kill it and it wouldn't die. And after getting out priorities straight, we resumed the activity and during the time we did not work our business, our income did not go down.

I believe, if we do it God's way, our health can and will improve. After 45 years of using the Shaklee Products I know I am healthier than I was 45 years ago, and I feel better too. Every Shaklee product is guaranteed so if you don't get the results you are looking for, you will get your money back.

Nutritional Health

I am happy to be your "guinea pig", so you know that the INTEGRITY of the Shaklee products is real and I believe, as close to the real thing (Nature) as we can get on the market today, they are designed that way.

So, I also give you permission to treat your body well, it is the only one you will have, and it has to house you (the real you) until you leave it here and move on...either up or down- your choice.

I am so convinced that I have been given a wonderful gift of health in a Country and World that is against it! My desire is that all of you will take this opportunity to at least try the Shaklee Products, and if you don't feel better in 30 days or less, you can send (even the empty container back) for a full refund.

If you call or text me, (301-580-2824) I can send you (via email or text) a health assessment (HealthPrint) that will guide you in what to try, for your own health. You can also go on my website: pws.Shaklee.com/healthierlife-4U

You have heard my heart; I have to share my passion. I really want you to have Jesus and Health (in that order). I don't wish to be younger, I felt bad then, most of the time. Old age is wonderful when your fit to do what God has called you to do, and you can enjoy it. Now I am **Flourishing to the Finish and loving' it! Ps 92:13-14**

I'm Grandma Swann, a 76-year-old Widow, born in Oregon, I spent 50 years in DC & MD, and I am full-time RV-ing, (Jesus & me), currently in Florida. I have a Stepdaughter, 4 Step Grandchildren, and two Step Great Grandchildren. (I never had children. I have a very large "adopted" Family (350 and counting). I am the owner and CEO of a thriving Shaklee business that my husband and I built, that has paid me every month, for 45 years, virtually on the business we generated our first month in July of 1974. I was married for 43 years to Rev. Floyd Swann, a wonderful, Godly man, who finished his course and went home to Jesus in 2012. I have been a Millionaire and down to 8 cents to my name and have been content in each of those states. I trust the Lord. I am medication free, debt free, stress free, house & stuff free, worry free, disease & pain free and intend to keep it that way! I'm in Christ Jesus! I am an example, and I desire everyone I meet or have met in my lifetime to have the same benefits.

I have a vision: To reach 100 million people, in my lifetime, with a way to freedom and independence from this worlds system.

I have a mission:
- I am a bridge, a connector of people and things.
- I am flourishing to the finish!
- Millionaire again by my 80th Birthday.
- Master Coordinator in Shaklee with 5,000 Leaders.
- Encourage everyone, that is drawn to me, by the Holy Spirit, to know the truth, fullness, peace, joy and know who they are in Jesus Christ
- I am passionate about the Vision, and my mission.

You are welcome to and encouraged to **join me** and the many others that agree, and have a heart for this hurting generation, and want to see all reach their full potential and maximize God's purpose and plan for their lives.

What steps are you willing to take to improve your nutritional health?

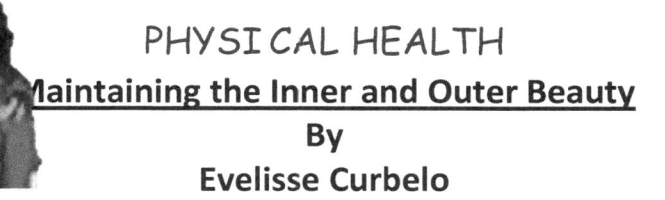

PHYSICAL HEALTH
Maintaining the Inner and Outer Beauty
By
Evelisse Curbelo

    I always knew who my dad was and where he lived, but he was not in my life. He had four other daughters and a wife, but he didn't really want me. It bothered me as a little girl because I could not understand why he didn't want me. At the age of thirteen, I remember getting on a train to go and see him. I remember ringing his doorbell and him not answering. I remember hearing voices of kids and others, but no one answered. It was April 5th, my birthday and my dad didn't want to know me or see me. He rejected me as he did over the years. I would always question if he truly loved his first daughter.

    When I graduated from the militarily, I wanted to show my dad my accomplishment to see if he would be proud of me. I remember pulling up in the parking lot and seeing my father, his wife, and my four sisters walking towards me. I got out of the car and he walked past me as if he didn't even see me and it hurt. I felt s rejected. Growing up without a father figure made me seek attention and love from older men. Because I was seeking that attention, I met the men who became my husband who is 21 years older than I am. He led me down the road to the party scene that involved drinking and drugs. This relationship also led me to discover healing in the physical and spiritual aspects. Although he led me down a path of destruction, he also taught me about proper nutrition and physical fitness. This is why I believe that God put him into my life to teach me and prepare me for the physical element in the future. So, it is true that He goes before you and make your path straight. He turned what the devil meant for evil for my good.

In 2010 I was working as a certified nursing assistant and one day my joints swelled up. I experienced depression, anxiety, and suicidal thoughts because there was no diagnosis of what was happening to me. After two years of joint pain, I moved to Florida and was blessed to find doctors that could put a name to my condition. Since 2012, I have tried multiple medications with no help or healing. I was forced to treat myself with holistic medicine. Although my condition is still visible, my mind, body has begun its healing process through eating right, exercising, and trusting God to deliver and heal me.

1Peter 3:3 Your beauty should not come from outward adornment, such as elaborate hairstyles and the wearing of gold jewelry or fine clothes. **4** Rather, it should be that of your inner self, the unfading beauty of a gentle and quiet spirit, which is of great worth in God's sight.

This scripture is not telling us that we should not care about how we look on the outside, or that we should not wear jewelry or makeup, but that it should not be our main focus. We should make sure that our inner beauty is intact before our outer beauty. You will see in scripture that women were outwardly beautiful, wore jewelry, and makeup. We need to focus on adorning ourselves with the fruit of the Spirit instead of the fruit of the flesh. They are in opposition to each other. If one is there, the other is not.

Inner beauty defines how attractive a person is to another. This is why sometimes you can see an accomplished man married to a woman who may be physically unattractive by the world's standards but is as kind and humble as ever. Are you kind? How are you as a person? Inner beauty is something that is widely undervalued and underestimated all over the word. Constant body shaming, keeping to a standard of a body image that is frequent in advertisements showing us images of perfection which keeps us from being who God designed us to be. When we ask someone to describe someone else, the attributes are usually physical. Is this what we should go by? God said to judge a person by their fruit. That he looks at a man's heart, but it us that looks at the outward appearance.

Fruit of the Spirit	Fleshly Desires
Love	Sexual Immorality
	Impurity
	Sensuality
	Orgies
	The Like
Joy	Enmity
Peace	Strife
Patience	Jealousy
	Envy
Kindness	Rivalry
Goodness	Dissensions
Faithfulness	Idolatry
	Sorcery
	Divisions
Gentleness	Fits of Anger
Self-Control	Drunkenness

Figure 4 Writings from eden. wordpress.c

We need to learn to be fruit inspectors. The fruit of the Spirit were mentioned earlier but here they are compared to the fruit of the flesh:

THE FLESH vs THE SPIRIT

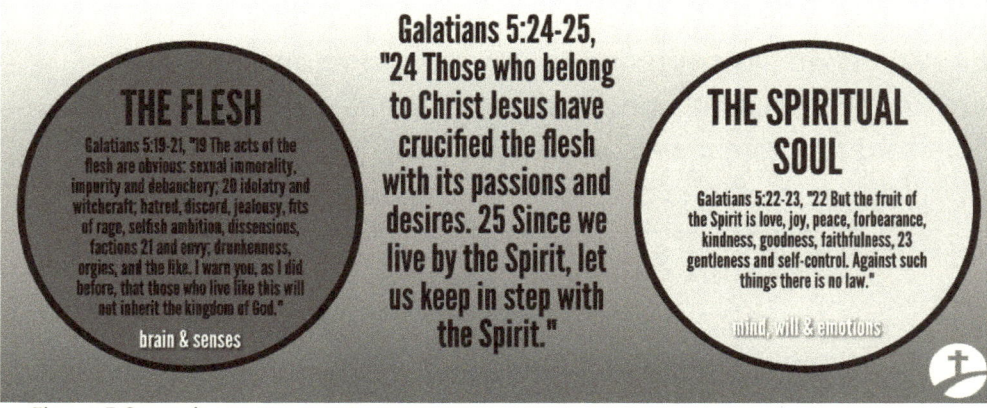

THE FLESH
Galatians 5:19-21, "19 The acts of the flesh are obvious: sexual immorality, impurity and debauchery; 20 idolatry and witchcraft; hatred, discord, jealousy, fits of rage, selfish ambition, dissensions, factions 21 and envy; drunkenness, orgies, and the like. I warn you, as I did before, that those who live like this will not inherit the kingdom of God."
brain & senses

Galatians 5:24-25, "24 Those who belong to Christ Jesus have crucified the flesh with its passions and desires. 25 Since we live by the Spirit, let us keep in step with the Spirit."

THE SPIRITUAL SOUL
Galatians 5:22-23, "22 But the fruit of the Spirit is love, joy, peace, forbearance, kindness, goodness, faithfulness, 23 gentleness and self-control. Against such things there is no law."
mind, will & emotions

Figure 5 Steemit.com

Today, many of us are so obsessed with having a perfect body image that we overlook that which brings life to our inner selves. The beauty standards of the world bring us sadness throughout our lives; creates negativity, displeasures, and discontentment with our lives and natural appearances. It hinders us from being confident and restrains us from bringing out our gifts and talents. By giving our appearance the number one priority shows that we are not trying to improve ourselves to become like Christ but trying to improve ourselves to look like the world. **We are just blending in instead of standing out.**

God called us to be a peculiar people. A royal priesthood. Royalty do not blend into culture, they make culture. They set the standard. They don't become like their subjects. They standout and apart so that their subjects will have a desire to become like them. So, which column do you tend to fall into more frequently? It's time to get to the roots and change the type of fruit you produce. It is time to change your tree.

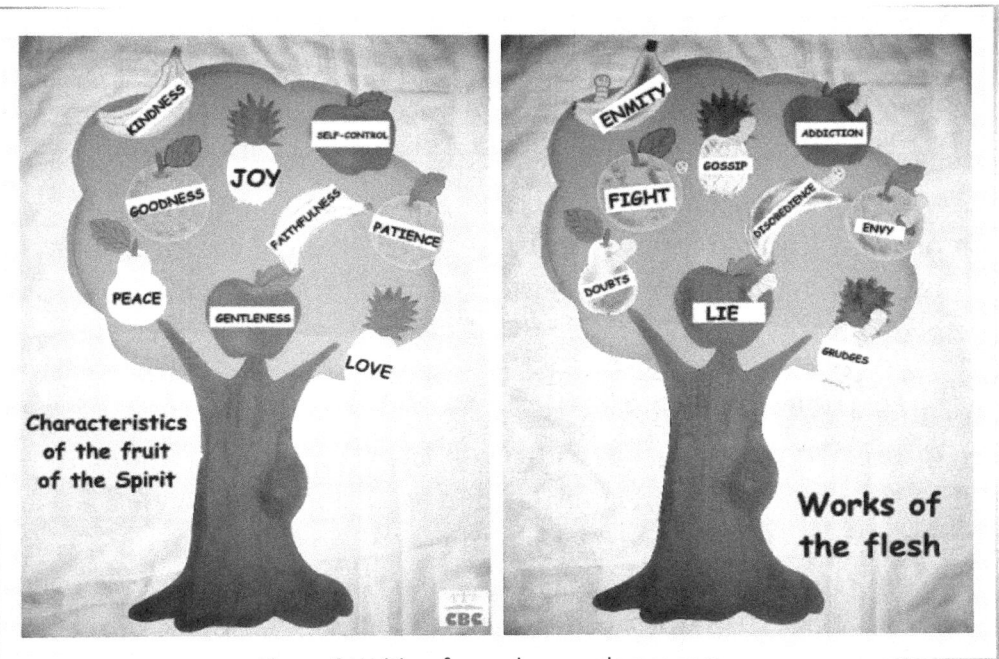

Figure 6 Writingsfromeden.wordpress.com

Now, does this mean we should walk around in baggy clothes hiding our God given curves, No. It means that we are not to put them on display. He does not women looking like men or men looking like women. It is a dishonor to his creation. If you change a Vincent van Gogh painting even just a little bit, it will lose its value. He was specific in making men and women differently. It was why in the beginning of creation He showed the differences in how we were made so that we would never become confused. He gave every male an "Adams" apple and a Y chromosome. A woman could never truly be a man nor a man a woman.

There is a need for exercise, but not to the point where a woman starts to look like a man. In Biblical days they walked everywhere they had to go or rode on animals. They had plenty of exercise. In order for is to have the stamina and endurance to do the work that God is calling us too for His kingdom, we need to incorporate daily exercise to keep us toned and in a healthy condition. Here are ways to incorporate daily physical fitness in the gym but can also be done in the home by being creative with chairs, steps, and can goods. The important thing is to ensure that each body part receives a day of exercise and that cardio is incorporated for warming up and improving the heart.

MAINTAIN YOUR PHYSICAL HEALTH

Optimizing your overall health will allow you to be your best self professionally, spiritually, and in your daily life. Over-exercising, lack of sleep, emotional stress, and occasionally consuming unhealthy foods can leave a body depleted. The more you allow healthy habits into your life, the closer you will be to living your best life.

PRE-WORKOUT:
- Prepare healthy fat, protein enriched foods for the entire week.
- Eat small portions every 2 hours (can consist of protein bars, drinks, or foods; should not exceed 3 meals and 2 snacks)
- Eat 100–200 calories of high-quality carbohydrates (sweet potatoes or brown rice) for every hour of exercise. This will give your body the fuel it needs without depleting its balance of nutrients, which can leave you feeling exhausted.

WORKOUT SCHEDULE

The following 5-day workout routine is based on a 5-day split. This routine is set up to train one body part per day for a duration of 5 days. There are two main advantages to using this type of routine.

1. You can train the body part for that day with all effort and intensity and you do not have to worry about training two or more body parts at the same time. It also allows you to do more sets and more exercises.

2. It will allow for a longer period of rest. Training one body part per week will allow maximum rest and your muscles have longer time to recuperation during body parts.

Note: You can either use one- or two-days rest at the end of the training week. I recommend two at first and as you progress, try using one day. However, you will have to "play it by ear" and listen to your body not everyone's body is the same.

Five Day Workout Schedule
Day 1 **Legs/Cardio**
Day 2 **Chest/Abs/Cardio**
Day 3 **Back/Cardio**
Day 4 **Shoulders/Abs/Cardio**
Day 5 **Triceps/Biceps/Cardio**
Day 6 **Rest/ Cardio Optional**
Day 7 **Rest/ Cardio Optional**

LEGS
Leg Press
Barbell Front Squat
Seated Leg Curl Machine
Seated Calf Raise Machine
Leg Extension Machine
Hip Abduction
Hip Adduction

Day 1 Legs

Exercise	Sets	Reps	Rest
Leg Press	4	15-20	1 Minute
Leg Extensions	4	15-20	1 Minute
Leg Curls	4	15-20	1 Minute
Hip Abduction	4	15-20	1 minute
Hip Adduction	4	15-20	1 Minuit
Calf Raises	4	15-20	1 Minute
Cardio		20-25 Minutes	

CHEST
Incline Dumbbell bench press
Incline bench press
Seated chest press
Cable crossover
Cable chest fly

Day 2 Chest

Exercise	Sets	Reps	Rest
Incline Dumbbell Press	4	15-20	1 minute
Seated chest press	4	15-20	1 minute
Cable chest fly	4	15-20	1 minute
Cable crossover	4	15-20	1 minute
Leg Raises	3	20-25	1 minute
Cable crunches	3	20-25	1 minute
Incline Sit ups	3	20-25	1 minute
Cardio		20-25	

BACK

Dumbbell Row
Seated Cable Row
hammer strength Row
Lat Pulldown Pendlay Row
Lower Back Hyperextension

Day 3 Back/Cardio

Exercises	Sets	Reps	Rest
One Arm Dumbbell Rows	4	15-20	1 minute
Seated Cable Row	4	15-20	1 minute
Pendlay Row	4	15-20	1 minute
Lat Pulldown	4	15-20	1 minute
Hammer Strength Row	4	15-20	1 minute
Cardio		20-25 Minutes	

SHOULDERS

Front Dumbbell Raises
Side dumbbell Raises
Overhead Press

Rear Delt Dumbbell Press
Rear Delt Machine Fly
Shrugs

Day 4 Shoulders

Exercises	Sets	Reps	Rest
Military Press	4	15-20	1 minute
Rear Delt Machine Fly	4	15-20	1 minute
Front Dumbbell Raises	4	15-20	1 minute
Side dumbbell Raises	4	15-20	1 minute
Shrugs	4	15-20	1 minute
Incline Sit ups	4	30-40	1 minute
Cardio		20-25 Minutes	

ARMS

Cable overhead extension
V-bar push down
Rope push down
Ring dip
Dumbbells Kick back
Barbell curls
Cable curls
Dumbbells curls
Seated incline Dumbbell curls
Dumbbell Hammer curl

Day 5 Arms/Cardio

Exercises	Sets	Reps	Rest
Rope push down	4	15-20	1 minute
Cable overhead extension	4	15-20	1 minute
Dumbbells Kick back	4	15-20	1 minute
Barbell curls	4	15-20	1 minute
Dumbbell Hammer curl	4	15-20	1 minute

POST WORKOUT

Recovery begins 30–60 minutes following a workout. Your body needs to be replenished and toxins flushed.

1. Use a foam roller to roll the scar tissue built up on your muscles.
2. Eat protein immediately to repair and rebuild during recovery, and carbohydrates to replace glycogen stores.
3. Drink an ounce of water for every pound of your weight per day: Proper hydration is needed to replenish, and fluids lost, and to flush away toxins.

Make time for proper rest with sleep, stretching, and meditation. When the body is stressed it produces a hormone called cortisol. Cortisol improves mood and can protect cells from stress damage. In excessive amounts, cortisol can cause you to feel confused, cause the body to store excessive fat. Pain and inflammation are reduced with proper rest.

1. <u>Stretching</u>: Stretching right after working out isn't only beneficial for general mobility.
2. <u>Sleep</u>: Most people need 8–10 hours of sleep every night.
3. <u>Meditation</u>: Keep this Book of the Law always on your lips; meditate on it day and night, so that you may be careful to do everything written in it. Then you will be prosperous and successful. Joshua 1:8
4. <u>Take nutritional supplements</u> to give your body all the nutrients it needs, even when the healthiest diet may be lacking:
   - Vitamin D: for healthy immune system function, bones and teeth.
   - Vitamin K: Supports healthy bones.
   - B Vitamins: For brain function, immune system activity, and converting fats and carbohydrates into energy.

- Chromium: For proper blood-insulin function.
- Selenium: Supports proper endocrine health.
- Molybdenum: For optimal immune function
- Trace Minerals: Lesser-known nutrients that support health

What are your plans to improve your physical health and other takeaways you may have?

Physical Health

THE CONCLUSION ON THE MATTER

There are no fingers being pointed here and no blame to cast. There was a fall of man and woman causing a man's servant leadership to be replaced with tyranny and a desire for power or by an indifference and unwillingness to offer spiritual leadership. Men became the helpers and the women became the headship. This can be changed by either party reversing the roles back. In loving headship, the man humbles himself to meet the needs of his wife; loving, submitting to, nourishing, and cherishing his treasure. A loving helpmeet humbles herself to meet the needs of her husband; respectful, submitting to him, and cooperative instead of stubborn. This reciprocal relationship says that a husband's loving headship awakens a responsive submission from the wife and the submissive cooperation from the wife draws sensitive leadership from her husband. Let the more mature one start.

A sensitive leader is in position to do right by his woman. Just as God made provision for a woman to be restored, a sensitive leader will understand the needs of his wife and give her what she needs. In Deuteronomy 21:10-14, you see God's provision for women:

¹⁰ "When you go out to war against your enemies, and the Lord your God gives them into your hand and you take them captive, **(This shows that he is a man of God. A man that listens to and hears from God. It shows that he has favor from God.)**

¹¹ and you see among the captives a beautiful woman, and you desire to take her to be your wife, **(He had to control his emotions. He couldn't just take her and rape her. He**

couldn't do with her as he pleased. He wasn't controlled or overcome by his lust or unnatural desires for a man.)

¹² **and you bring her home to your house, she shall shave her head and pare her nails. (He provided for her the things she needed to care for herself and to clothe herself. He humbled himself to meet the needs of her so that she could reach her full spiritual potential. He didn't have to feel the shame of not being able to provide for her.)**

¹³ And she shall take off the clothes in which she was captured and shall remain in your house and lament her father and her mother a full month. After that you may go into her and be her husband, and she shall be your wife. **(He protects her and treats her as an equal but weaker vessel allowing her to become whole before making her his wife. He did not treat her like an object or a slave, he held her in a high position as wife.)**

¹⁴ But if you no longer delight in her, you shall let her go where she wants. But you shall not sell her for money, nor shall you treat her as a slave, since you have humiliated her. **(Finally, he followed God's design for masculinity. He couldn't just move on with his life doing what he wanted to do while still being married to her. He had to set her free giving her full control over herself. He could only approach her as a husband with full respect of her womanhood.)**

We have been trying so long to make God fit into our ideas of religion and identity. That we forgot that he designed us, made provision for us to protect us from the hurt he knew people would inflict on us, and provided a way for us to be restored and reconciled back to Him.

We use legalism as way to exalt ourselves by following strict rules and regulations. We use propositionalism making God seem rigid and fixed. Putting Him in our boxes of what He would or would not do to justify we are who we are. We use secularism to make ourselves comfortable living outside of what God says is okay or not okay. Saying things like it is legal for a man to marry a man or a woman to marry a woman and so we have to follow those rules or that God is okay with abortion. We know that God opposes those things, but we trick ourselves.

God wants to tend to the individual details that restores you. Somehow you got stuck in the curse. You separated yourself from your natural feminine or masculine traits and accepted life as usual. Being a man was too hard, being a woman caused too much trauma. Someone used your vulnerability against you and now you are operating out of the curse. Your life is filled with worry, health problems, anxiety, and walls around your heart. (Pro 14:1) You think you have walled of the hurt that can get to you, but you really have walled in the bitterness, the pain, and the suffering and no one can get in to help.

You have overcome, but you overcome with bitterness. You went through but left you somewhere. Those who overcome trials and tribulations and still be soft gentle creatures excel in the area of strength and weakness. You have a façade of holiness to avoid feeling vulnerable or to mask the laziness. Gen 3:7 They hid behind a façade of their own making because of their shame. At the beginning of the hurt you had a choice to accept God's grace or to become bitter. Accept His grace now. Some of you are stuck in legalism (following rules and regulations in hopes of changing), propositionalism (rigid or fixed in your faith that God can only do one thing and not another. Or that a strong woman cannot be a soft woman), and secularism (what the world says we are supposed to be and do).

God said to come out and come out now. He is the author and the finisher of this design. He created them, male and female, he created. Not man for woman but woman for man. We do not get to decide what gender we take. It was decided in the womb. It is time to be healed from the bitterness and rebellion against being a woman or man. It is time to forgive and be forgiven.

Who do you need in order to move forward? What are your next steps?

Goal Planning

Setting Goals

Something I want to accomplish in the next week:

In the next month:

In the next year:

In five years:

Obstacles and Strategies

Obstacles to reaching my goals:

Things I will need to do to achieve my goals:

What I can begin doing tomorrow to work toward my goals:

Goal Planning

Setting Goals

Something I want to accomplish in the next week:

In the next month:

In the next year:

In five years:

Obstacles and Strategies

Obstacles to reaching my goals:

Things I will need to do to achieve my goals:

What I can begin doing tomorrow to work toward my goals:

ABOUT VIRTUOUS BY DESIGN

VirtuousByDesign.org

Our mission is to empower women to discover and fulfill their Christ ordained purpose.

PURPOSE:
-to love God
-love self and others
-make disciples

Called-Chosen-Changed-Treasured-Set Free

We support women at every stage of their life, from teenage puberty through post-menopausal. We tackle issues, such as bullying, addiction, suicide, mental illness, identity crisis, etc. with:

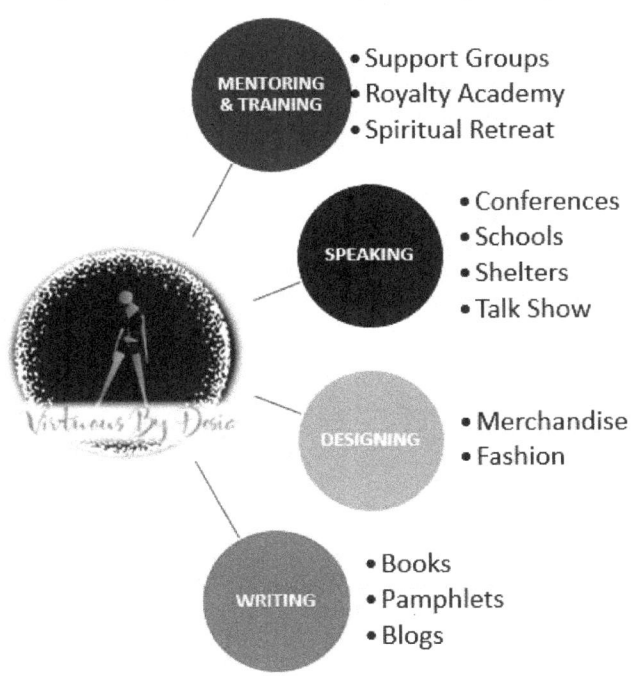

MENTORING & TRAINING
- Support Groups
- Royalty Academy
- Spiritual Retreat

SPEAKING
- Conferences
- Schools
- Shelters
- Talk Show

DESIGNING
- Merchandise
- Fashion

WRITING
- Books
- Pamphlets
- Blogs